"Steve Goldberg is a poet of bakeries and breakups, rainy days and buried memories. Like all good poets, he pays attention. He's obsessed with the ordinary and the overlooked. He's the poet next door who goes to the corner bar. He's a poet who pauses during the day because he knows that, "I'm in the three o'clock of my life / And it's three o'clock in the afternoon.""

-Mike James, author of *Crows in the Jukebox*

"Into a world increasingly inundated with words of polish and spin, vetted and cleared for the duty of obstructing truth and beauty, come these poems — giving us the unglossed, unvarnished truth of the human heart. And for that, the reader can be thankful."

-Milenko (Miles) Budimir, author of *Departures* and *Rustbelt Romance*

"Steve Goldberg doesn't care if you see him in his robe. He won't change for you, and he pays the price. He's an observer, from his city to the room behind his reflection in the mirror. He is a poet who examines context. He knows how he got here. He knows how we got here."

-Elynn Alexander, publisher at Collapse Press and author of *The Shouldspeak Disease*

History is an Afterthought

Poems by Steve Goldberg

Luchador Press

Big Tuna, TX

This book would never have been possible without the advocacy and guidance of John Dorsey and the great wisdom of Jason Ryberg to agree with him. They have both been friends of mine for many years, and have my undying gratitude. I also want to thank Claire McMahon and Miles Budimir for the support, inspiration, and encouragement that let this tech head reach for literary stars for a change. My education in poetry writing was enhanced by the regular members in various workshops in Cleveland, specifically those run by above mentioned Claire and Ray McNiece, the Rufus by Wendy Shaffer, and the casual readings organized by Russell Vidrick and now past friends Jim Lang and Maj Ragain. I would be remiss to also thank all my literally hundreds of siblings in verse from around the country and few beyond, for the inspiration and comradery at the various poetry festivals I was able to attend. I hope you all enjoy this work.

The following poems have appeared in various forms previously:

"My Perch," "Life in A Hood in Cleveland," "Magic,"
"Neighbor," "Tremont Summer Storm," *Tremont Crawl*
    (WhatsInTheBag Press)
"Tremont Summer Storm," / *Animals without Backbones*
    (Green Panda Press)
"Its always 3 o' clock," "Slouch Hat" / *The Brandt Gallery
    21st Anniversary Anthology,*
"Las Palomas" / *Corner Café Drugstore and Other Poems*
    (Inkstained Dagger Press),
"Book By It's Cover" / *The City Press #18,*
"Eventually" / *Hessler Street Fair Poetry Anthology 2008,*
"Good Will to Some Men" / *Bag-o-zine 65* (Split Whiskey),
"Nothing Else I Can Do" / *Cleve on Cleve* (Green Panda
    Press),
"Visit Home" / *Hessler Street Fair Poetry Anthology 2010,*
"Walts Beard" / *Polarity eMagazine* (Poetry Bay),
"With Success" / *Red Fez #35*

TABLE OF CONTENTS

We have all had at least that one teacher that made a huge impact on our lives. My teacher for 10th grade AP English was one of mine. On a test in early American literature, she gave me exactly zero credit for my interpretation of a five line Emily Dickenson poem. An INTERPRETATION, mind you, which put me off of poetry for more than 20 years. Therefore, Mrs. Estelle Koski, dead or alive, this book is to you, a big Fuck You.

History is an Afterthought

Oh! Sweet Child!

You are too young to have a face that old.
Not like a crone old, with face
lined by wrinkles of experience.
No, when you strolled down the aisle
and looked at me at the sandwich shop,
those dimples in your suntanned cheeks
exploded when you smiled,
Your full lips should not spread into that duplicitous
    shy smile
or your head nods in acknowledgement of a shared
    secret.

But those eyes, blue as a rare Cleveland cloudless sky,
sparkled when they caught me chewing a mouthful.
Knowing eyes, like they perused with crow feet
    understanding
Nabokov's scandalous manuscript,
are too mature for your four & half foot frame.

My muse, my angel of flip flops & sundresses,
stay young and don't let age dull
your sun streaked hair.

Never Alone

Friends worry as I rattle about
inside my apartment,
alone lesson of relationship gone its course,
mumbling to myself with an occasional chuckle
They must think I'm losing it,
too long alone, need a woman,
or a pet since they're not so picky.
They are so kind, but way off track.

How can I be alone?
I heard the neighborhood dogs
bark yapping at pedestrians, real and imagined,
the robin family squatters in the eave,
the street kids goofing and laughing
to pass the hot summer evenings.

I don't like to use the phone.
Don't know why, I've been that way since I was a kid.
Must be why friends want me to have a chatting pal.
They know I like face-to-face, mano-a-mano discourse.
They want me to have someone to listen to me
instead of air.
That's what they think is loneliness.
That's where they track the wrong trail.

I read that talking to God is not a waste of time.
He/she may not talk back, but is listening
while running the show.

NSA collects my phone records, for what its worth.
AT&T announces they own my personal data and
    can do what they please.
Good thing the info is only about me and not me,
else I'd feel owned,
although I sense cat5, 24 gauge, and red tape enwrapping
    like chains.

God makes things work while listening.
Corporo-gov't listens while futzing things up.
There is some confusion
God-Gov't, Gov't-God
Guess who has it right.

Any wonder I chuckle
while others surreptitiously listen to me,
guessing about BuJu babblings
confusing the confused State-Church Industrial
    inferiority complex
Is it lonely snickering when I'm so amused?

Nothing Else I Can Do

(for Terry Provost)

We know, together
What is really happening in your head
We spent part of our career, together
To see and treat what is in your head
But blinking lights and invisible rays
Sterilized gowns, expensive equipment
and the paperwork
oh the paperwork
segregated the growing demons
the parasite made from ourselves, but not ourselves
what older people still whisper "the C"
We worked and created way to find and view
The creature that lurks within
But that was a long time ago
Before they said we weren't needed
To forge the weapons
To fashion the armor
To do battle
Not anymore

Now it has tracked us down
Revenge impels its wanton growth spurts
infiltrated in your head,
the place that generated so many obstacles to its plan
for human domination
Now the place that conjures poetic spells
to enlighten listeners

to the injustices by our government
to point at the absurdity of our society
to see the love of friends
and the sweet grace of a son

It attacked you but I feel the pain
The pain from knowing I deserve as much
For my part in the war against disease
The pain of dodging the bullet
The pain of not having the old tools anymore
The old weapons the old armor
To fight on your behalf
The pain of helplessness

So all I can do is hug you.

Procrastination

Rainy Sunday mornings are made for poetry reading
    in a lounge chair.
Not the famous ancient poets of civilization building
as teachers and professors
adjudicated for yawning adolescents
in forced indoctrination sessions, chained
to desks without room for modern knees.

No, Sunday mornings are for friends' words
acquaintances met once at a show
with beer or espresso or both,
or for names recognized or recommended
by the wise street educated.

Poems about dreams, blood, death, love,
and the opposite of love.
Silence interrupted by sips of coffee,
the pit-pat of errant raindrops on a window,
the occasional fart, or chuckle, or sob.

A world where words are simultaneously seen
with images of mundane livingroom clutter
and imagined vignettes of fancy
maybe blurred by empathetic tear
whether of grief or joy.

Reading in comfort in order to be
uncomfortable.

Reading to rediscover the kick in the gut
and hunger of emptiness
and feel the need to stop procrastinating.
The responsible conscience whispering it awake
between page turns.
Says to get dressed and get ready for chores.
Grudgingly, the book is closed, but the lessons
are remembered.
But the already put off chores can wait a bit longer
for you to finish writing in a fresh new notebook,
proud to use procrastination to fight
procrastination.

Book By Its Cover

Usually when I order a book
a poetry book
from the public library,
it arrives pristine.
Covers still shiny
with publisher gloss.
The spine would crack
with excess glue
when opened.

No one reads poetry anymore
At least from a public library.

But the Bukowski books
come like they stayed with Hank
in the tarpaper shack in Atlanta
was his pillow on the park bench.
Even the ones published after his death.

I've read four Buk books in three weeks
2 novels, his first and his last
a compilation of letters from a seven-year love affair
a middle-aged drunk and a hot avant-garde chick
separated by only 350 miles
yet never met.
And a book of poems.

Maybe it was in an inspired dream
cuz I can't find it in any of these tomes,
but thus I have heard Hank say
the world is created by what we perceive,
who we are,
so the critics that see that we are in a shithole
should know
that they are the main turds.

Maybe that's why
the books I get
are worn, dog-eared,
re-covered with
original titles cut-out,
pasted to the front and spine.
People who go to public libraries
want to read that.

Buk Lessons

I think I know what it is about Bukowski that appeals
to me. He has a lesson. That women who are attracted to fat
old men, especially the young ones, are crazy. Yet Why do
I want to have such a one like that.
Maybe because I'll be the special one. I'm not as ugly as
Buk, or as fat. I'm not as grumpy though I want my peace.
I'm also not as talented.
Hank is warning me, but I 'm not as smart as he is either

and I think I have to find out for myself.

Walt's Beard

When I was ten or eleven,
I sat with an ice cream
at a picnic table next to a cabin
that was Walt Whitman's birthplace.
I wondered if his beard was born there too,
such a tiny place and such an enormous beard.

I was a fan of Abraham Lincoln
since I was him in a first grade play.
We sang George M. Cohan songs.
The teacher read "O Captain, My Captain."
I knew if Whitman liked Abe
as much as that,
he was alright with me.

I licked my ice cream cone quickly
to prevent drips on the leaves of grass.
I wondered if Walt liked ice cream too.
He must have if he liked Lincoln.
But how did he eat it with that
wonderful
magnificent
beard?

The Ugly Truth

Why is Truth always so ugly?
What was Keats talking about:
>   "Beauty Truth, Truth Beauty.
>   That is all you know
>   That is all you need to know."
Every time Truth is revealed to me
it pulls the rug from under my feet
The North Star blinks from 10 different directions.
My handholds dissolve into pondscum.
My feet are either
mired in quicksand
or slide as if on super-slippery ice.

No, Truth, as I ever found it,
tears reality to shreds
leaves acid clouds to burn my soul.
It rips off masks, leaving demon grimaces,
strips shades from windows inviting
blinding, disorienting brightness.
It shorns the hair off of supermodels
leaving nothing to the imagination.

Truth breaks mirrors,
then pops out our eyes,
then shoves them back into our heads
backwards.

There, we see what is really behind all the fuss.
It is a scary place
>   and with us all the time.

History is an Afterthought

We get together, at first,
to listen to each other's words
at an open mic or a workshop.
We glean, like from a wheat field,
the essence of what is important
what makes each of us tick
if we are honest.
We all have bullshit detectors
so sensitive
no one gets by.
We know each other and we hang with each other
most of all, we like each other
and we talk
talk of poetry, of course,
talk of personal importance
talk of social ills and of what we would change
if we were more than just poets.
We would share stories outside of our writings
of writers we know or have not.
Some are famous
or were famous
or only famous in their neighborhood.
Pictures of us hanging together
at a restaurant or a bar
or at a reading of an influence.
We don't care, we only love the word
and each other.

But sometimes
as books of literary history
are perused
and pictures of the now famous
are scrutinized,
the question is begged:
Did they know they would be a school?
Did they know they would be famous?
Did they know?
We don't know,
but do we care?

Galatia

Wacky sleep patterns cause wakefulness at odd hours.
The amount of sleep actually had does not enter into the
  equation.
But one night, I found a benefit as I awoke at about
  5:30am.
Birds serenaded me to that in-between consciousness
where wonderful, lucid half-dreams
entertain me and sometimes inspire the seed to some of
  my favorite poems.

Begrudgingly, I arose to replenish the water lost
from the previous day's time in the sun.
In the still dark apartment,
the most magnificent golden glow greeted me in the
  kitchen.
This unexpected beauty had me wonder
if I was still asleep and in a very lucid dream.
Half expecting the flesh to be eaten away like in some
  twisted Twilight Zone episode,
I put my hand into the glow.
Instead, out of the black, white, and gray background
My skin looked more alive with technicolor fantasy.

I had to find out the source of the light.
I tracked it to an incredible single early morning sunrise ray.
It entered from just a tiny crack in the closed window
  shade my front room.

It floated over bachelor pad clutter and chaos
ignoring all the possible items
that could scatter, reflect, or interrupt
its path to the kitchen.

A silly solar-powered dancing hula girl trinket
was in the glow
and she slowly wiggled her plastic hips
from the miniscule real world power bolstered by an
    artful power.
She was Galatia, alive and dancing to greet the sun,
and I began to sway and twirl with her in this pagan
    celebration of a new day.

Her plastic smile seemed to grow broader
as I joined her in that simple and graceful motion,
bathing in the glorious glow of a golden sun

I smiled for hours long after the magic
and into the gentle rain that fell that magical Sunday morning.

Visit Home

Thru the rusted open gate
irises bend over, their beauty too heavy a burden,
the grass was recently mown
but not today.
Where is the lamb?

Bright green patches in the yard
create a verdant cheetah skin rug.
A few flowers sprout
in spots where the lamb left patties.
But where is the lamb?

The nuzzled nose in the crook of an arm,
the soft fleece gentle on the cheek
the pink tongue tickling the ear
the quiet bleat lulling the afternoon nap.
The lamb is gone,
memories are left.

The sun winks and clouds grin
at the fenced-in pasture.
Each time eyes land
on another green spot,
disappointment slaps the face
and sadness, sadness
pricks the heart.

The lamb is gone
and memory
avoids the thought
that it was me
who left the gate open
so long ago.

Waiting

My heart is of stone,
Stone –cold,
Stone silent,
Stone hard
with micro-cracks along its surface.
Waiting for the next blow
to crumble it into dust
or to release it from prison.

Tremont Summer Storm

Trio tall towers stand above the fray
Blinking lights signifying
great gold gusts of the past
or present pyrite instead

Nature's blowing blasts bending branches
of obscuring shrubs
heralding the coming of the Queen.

Looking upward toward the North
from my balcony flapping with flags
colors holding prayers carried by windhorses,
lightning flashes reflect on the Triplets.
Oblivious in the arrogant calm near the lake
angry clouds pushing from
the South roar:
"Listen to the Queen, Dammit"
to no avail.
Instead the tinkling of the wind chime fills the air
with hope of a cooling rain
to wash the angst from this lonely perch
Another promise unmet.

Unheeded by the mighty Three
the insulted royal Queen rolls east
looking for a more deserving court.
Leaving only a shower of few drops

as a calling card to remember her,

as if to say "I'll be back"

And I remain sweating on the stoop, looking North.

Life in a Hood of Cleveland

Only here in the "trendy'" part of the city
can a recently unemployed (unemployable)
hipster loving verse-engineer
wander into a hundred year old church
to watch modern dance.
Later, a stroll into a bar will bring maestro guitar
of jazz and blues.
Across the street a band banging out indy covers and
original tunes entertain the working masses.
The unemployed are welcome,
everybody there was in the same spot one time or another.
A bought beer to offer condolence and celebration
tastes sweet, as sweet the previous year when
roles were reversed.
Any other city would kick an ass
throw an Insult
or worse
ignore and add another to the non-person list.
But why ponder the misfortune that is not ours
Here in the Mont of trees
love abounds and art hold close
those aesthetes, though dollar deprived
still find the way to appreciate the intangible.

Sweet Egg Bread

I miss mallorca. That sweet
bread pastry introduced in Puerto Rico,
not by new and future ex-wife,
by her mother-not-mother.
What is Spanish for step-mother?
Everyday sent down 2 blocks
past semi-ornate iron grates
needed even on squalid concrete
homes in the tiny island
version of suburb.

The yellow bread, golden brown on top
sprinkled with powdered sugar.
Wonderful breakfast chew
when washed down with café con leche
or used in afternoon Cubano
or jamon y queso sandwiches.

The proprietor gazed at the macchiato
milky dollop, the lone blanco face floating
among the mulatto crowd of impatient mixed-Americans
that pledge allegiance to their Island.

Doña Rosa thought that this errand
will help learn Spanish, though the
peer pressured confusion took
the tongue and voice at the first
sound of "¿Que?"

The squeek of heavily non-native accented
"Sies Mallorca, por favor."
Brings an eye-rolled smile and
fast speech to her coworkers.

"¿Quanto?" invites a quick blurt
of syllables and
an embarrassed "Huh?"
And the kind baker says
slowly, deliberately in non-Hispanic fashion
"Seeks dōlrs eh sistee fife scents."
With the change comes the traditional
white bakery box, strung together
with red and white string
harking back to Shaefer's in long ago New York.
Whiffs of saliva generating aroma
arise thru the seams
giving promise of an authentic
Puerto Rican delight.

For a brief time, in hometown Cleveland,
at Lorelei's, home of the best flan
this side of Miami,
Ponce born baker
briefly had mallorca available.
But snow blinded Ohioans
without the pulse of palm trees in their hearts
ignored them. And softness turned to Akron rubber
when this gringo found them.

He chewed
and chewed
and chewed,
hoping to regain the goodness he remembered,

Without the same context, others inevitably
had the same jaw exercising experience
and so
no one bought,
and they disappeared,
extinct from the display case.

Missing the sun warmed salt spray smell of the breeze.
Missing the unconditional love from mother-in-law to
    bewildered mainlander.
Missing the salsa swing in my soul.
Missing my wife of 8 years' smooth stroke on my face
and
missing the magic mallorca while sipping con leche on
    west 25th street.

With Success

With success
comes expectation of success
but success slides in through the backdoor
ignoring all the conventions of polite company.
It comes suddenly, without knocking.
It knocks over vases and spills milk.

Expectation demands re-creation
of the unplanned,
of the unconventional,
that, which cannot be manufactured.
It shows itself
obnoxious,
rude,
a fat hobo at the backdoor,
hands out, stinking of itself, hate in its eyes.

It is pressure
and more expectation.
An expectation that kills its parents,
destroys the good
that generated success in the first place.

So success is a failure
and it's easier to skip to the end.
close the lights
light a cigarette
sip a beer
and check the lock on the backdoor.

Treasured

I keep trying to summarize
people and places
events and times
in the simplest easiest terms.
I stare thru them like they are a piece of glass,
clear and with smooth predictable parallel sides

They are rubies,
emeralds, sapphires
gems with facets
light bouncing
around them, inside them,
out of them

I try to shave with Occam's razor,
but I get cut
and the stubble remains.

The Details

I sit in my comfy chair,
legs wrapped in a blanket,
steamy coffee in a cup
as I am wont to do on wintry Sunday mornings.

In the silence, caffeine slaps my mind
in the rump and it goes
hither and thither into dusty corners
and opens dark boxes packed with
thoughts too frustrating or sad
and thoughts just needing
more time to cipher out.

Things like why no new significant writing has occurred,
so difficult and annoying.
The excuses come and they are so lame
I look at the cluttered room and start
filling a new box with lists of chores and tasks
that should be done soon
and promised pro bono work for friends.
After another sip, I'm overwhelmed
by the "to do"s and grasp the lazy procrastination
of the comfy chair and warm comforter.

I hold on to the desire to write but still don't write.
A two month old "Poets & Writer" magazine on the
end table falls into my lap. Quick flips
open to an article about Not Writing.

Gene Fowler explains why, "Writing is easy. All you do is
stare at a blank piece of paper until drops of blood
form on your forehead"

But then, Jimmy
Breslin explains, " I look for the dust in the air for that is
where words live tumbling lazily, remaining
just out of reach, and staying there, staying, staying,
staying, until something, an unseen waft of air
causes them to drift right up to your reach, gather
into sentences, one sentence, two sentences, that's
all you need to get started."
You have the most beautiful ugly mug, Jimmy.
I look up smiling, nodding, yes that's the way.

I see my space heater in the middle
of the room. a refurb bargain from Sharper Image.
I notice a missing
sliver of plastic from a corner. A detail missed
for a year, the essence of a bargain.

Glancing only a few degrees higher
on the far wall, a smudge on white. But
wait, are those are legs. Long legs of a Daddy Long Legs
spider. How long has he been there (my pet
that needs no cave) A picture of life, static
in the winter cold. A detail that keeps the apartment
free of pests.

Looking down a sheet of paper on the floor
listed all the contests I was to send my manuscript,
the precursor to mailed rejections.
Contest deadlines that recently passed,
a detail missed on the calendar

On another table a precarious tower
of bottle caps from beers sipped weeks ago.
Ballantine Ale rebuses left unsolved, medallions of
confusion that make sense now eyes are clear
and hieroglyph details identified.

I see a dust mote in the winter sunshine drift past
the solitary spider to alight on the space heater.
I pick up my pen and smile.
It is all in the details and start scribbling these words
using the magazine as a desk.

That Guy in the Bathrobe

Every neighborhood's got one,
The weird guy that leaves his house in a bathrobe.
He goes out late in the morning
or sometimes mid afternoon.
If it was only early morning,
no one would call him weird.
He scampers out his door
to pick up the mail
or move the garbage cans.
Sometimes, he just steps out past his porch,
looks around,
up to the sky,
and breathes,
deeply
and usually
he smiles for just being alive.
He'll wave at any gawkers
before trundling back to his front door,
maybe scratching something
his ass
his crotch
his head.

There is another person in the neighborhood
who also leaves the privacy of home and hearth,
but no one thinks she's weird.

She is a Hispanic lady that holds her head
up in that regal Latin way.
She wears a housecoat instead of ratty bathrobe.
She strides confidently in feathery slippers
and sometimes a hairnet or scarf.
She does not acknowledge anybody
Stays to her task of picking up the morning paper.
She quickly returns to her abode, scratching
nothing.
She only does this early mornings.
That must be why no one thinks her weird.

Our friend wears moccasins that flop
if the sinew shoestrings are untied.
Never a hairnet.
Sometimes he wears sweatpants under the robe,
sometimes not.
We hope he keeps his hands in his robe pockets
so an unexpected wind gust doesn't give us a surprise.
There is always suspense if he sees someone and pulls a hand
out to wave.

I saw him again this morning
and, yeah, I thought he was definitely weird
as I stared at him
in the mirror.

The Best

So evasive is the meaning of Life.
Philosophers and holy men have parlayed
the question into essays, books
and hours long discussions.
Questions into questions
Answers into questions
never questions into answers.

It's a good gig and would go far
with the right kind of marketing.
And better still with slick and subtle sales.
The marketers and the salesmen are pretty good,
excellent in fact.
With a bad product, nothing is wrong.

Perhaps that
is the answer,
the meaning.

No matter what we are dealt
good,
bad,
neutral.

Meaning is from finding
that thing of which
we are excellent.

My Secret Freedom

Now everyone has gone
and I walked around the cabin naked.
Barefoot and bare assed
I climbed all the stairs.
I explored everybody's room
with a sly smile knowing nobody would even suspect.
After a shower, I scratched my balls,
pleased with myself that I can do that and Joni can't.
I looked around for a full length mirror
and found it in my own shared room.
I pretend I am William Carlos Williams and did a Danse Russe
with my tee-shirt as partner.
After dressing, I took a shit with the bathroom door open.
Then I walked the grounds wishing it was warmer, so I could
continue my nude revolt.
Instead, I found a grasshopper reposed on the bunkhouse lock,
and giddily had to tell him what I just did.
He just stared at me as if to say
"So what, I do that every day."

So I got out this typewriter to write this poem.
I never could keep a secret.

Straight and Narrow

When promising to be Buddhist,
there are certain expectations.
There are vows that can be taken,
if wished.

Buddhist vows are funny.
If they can be easily, effortlessly kept,
all the time,   forever,
they don't mean much.

If it is hard
doubtful of success,
they help.
Help improve the quality of life.
Help make better people.
They have value because
they can be bent or broken.
Buddhist vows for the unordained
are simple, really.

Promise not to kill,
easy if for human death
not so easy for buggy death.
Promise not to steal,
also easy if the value isn't too high.
Promise not to lie,
the big ones like being enlightened or claiming to fly.

Also easy.

Promise not to have sexual misconduct, whatever that is.

> Maybe as long as nobody gets hurt from the rocks off,
> it's okay.
> Forced celibacy protects.
> Not sure if hurt by it.... yet.
> Check again in a while.

Promise not to take intoxicants,

traditionally.

Easy to bust, so hedged.

Try: not to GET intoxicated.

Very hard when hanging with poetic hipsters and academics,

I do okay, but sometimes slip with new friend

Jameson of the brown tears,

called spirits that add spirit

to my unbalanced elements.

Thanks, Maj, and damn you.

After a slip up,

> the get up,

the dust off and say oops.

Promise to do better next time

live with the hangover.

Met a young man today.

His vow is pure, no hedge.

Horse was his chosen ride,

but his oops   is his corpse.

Quite a determination

for one so young, twenty-one.

So earnest, but traveling the same mountain road
rocky with twists and turns
barefoot, no steed
learning of himself
like me.
learning of others
like me.
I'm on the inside lane.
safe when I slip.
He is on the outside
next to the ravine.

Slouch Hat

If only I could pull this slouch hat
over my ears,
past my chin,
over my chest,
then squeeze it over my beer bloated belly.

Then all anyone would see
is this big slouch hat.
No grey hair, jiggly jowls,
crow's feet, pimply nose
arthritic fingers, or
bloodshot eyes.

Nor a tear-streaked cheek.

Just a big slouch hat
Saying beautiful things
And they would love it.

Selective Hearing

Convulsing with economic shivers,
I recall my medical exam.
Necessary for acceptance
into indentured servitude.
they probe and poke
pull fluids from
your desperate body.
Maybe they won't find
any of the things you used to cope.
Then, they put headphones on you
and you hope for a rock concert
or you worry that it is part
of the reprogramming
to make you compliant to new authority
like in a sci-fi movie.

Instead beeps,
high and low,
left and right,
loud and soft,
cascade into your ears,
creating dizzying sequences
that turn reality into a question.

The doc informs me that I have
lower than normal hearing perception,

not from experimental noise show cacophony,
nor from diving expeditions, deeper than judicious.
Just normal across the board hearing loss from age
like when I shout at Dad to get some attention.

Yet, I still suspect that
all those beeps and buzzes
injected subliminal messages into my brain.
Maybe to make me more attentive
to the electronic beeps and buzzes
of modern office technology.
Perhaps, since I can no longer
understand conversations
with loud background music
or hubbub drone of other talk.

But then in the after hours,
happy hours,
maybe on a bar patio,
or on a balcony,
or by an open window,
or at a sidewalk café,
I hear the soft clicks of sparrow beaks
eating a discarded tortilla chip,
and the chittering of squirrels
as they find last year's nut stash.
Children laughing in a far off park,
and the yawning moan of a dog lazing in the sun.

Later, I see that I missed three phone calls,
two text messages,
and a voicemail.
I never heard the cellphone at all.

Schrödinger's Lottery Ticket

I had $5 dreams folded neatly in my pocket.
It is a colored piece of paper
with Five sets of five numbers
and an extra for each.
And I've carried it around for weeks
A big sign said that it could be worth
$133 million dollars.
Crazy money that could cure some headaches
And hide a trail or two.

The Hope in my pocket sent a little humming feeling
to my gut like the a pleasant little buzz
of a bee making honey
and spreading the warmth of limoncello after a full meal.
Yup, held that slip of paper for weeks now
and the buzz is still there.

It is funny how a simple change of a number
can shift an outlook,
incremented or decremented,
Still, if it resets to a single digit,
Somebody is a winner., somewhere.
More money than they could possibly
spend, if they were sane.
But they are probably mad, or will be soon.
Jesus or Moses may have performed miracles
like the coincidental selection of six numbers.
They may have been mad too.

I avoid those highway signs and convenient store posters
for as long as I can.
Don't read newspapers or listen to local radio
to protect that little buzz.
But it was millions of little bright lights
on a faraway billboard
that evaporated the giddy Mystery like dew in the sun.
Somebody is a winner., somewhere.

The billboard shattered probability into reality
like listening for cat's breath
through a box.
Or for me,
looking at that bright sign,
I smelt the rising stench of decay
from that same box closed for far too long.

Neighbor

I hate you for fucking around with the garbage
and always leaving the can by my door.
For filling it with bulky inconsequential things that
leaves no room for my bags.
I hate you for a dog that never stops yapping.
for always leaving him out our back yard shitting wherever
and not picking up after him.
I hate you for slamming your doors
that shake my pictures on the wall awry,
that startles me out of' sleep,
just to let the little yipper out to
shit on my green splendor some more.
I hate you for the boyfriend that parks too close to my car,
for the fact that you get fucked by him most every night
    you want.

I hate you for your youth.
but I can't be a dick and so I'll shovel your stairs
and shovel a walk to your car
so you can go to work
or school
or wherever you go
or your boyfriend goes
in the morning
when I don't have any place to be.

Magic

A tree branch outline
in front of a hundred year old church
glows white.
An overhead street lamp
illuminates
it just so.
The magic like from a cartoon is here,
alive in three dimensional madness.
And then to see in a small triangle of light,
why magic exists.
Invisible snow blows in large clumps ,
alive and dancing in glee of pure existence.
It is like it's trying to show
me, especially me,
the one that happens to be staring out
that window
that particular time
and that sees what is going on in appreciative amazement.

Yes,
that's what I want to share with loves
of the past and why I want love in the future.
It is too much to keep to myself.
Even a loner wants happiness,
to touch others.
Maybe next time, I will have someone with me
to show

how fog and smoke
act like urban fairies
when light hits it just so
and we look
from
just
right
here.

Love Poem to a Friend

Somehow you became my dearest and closest friend.
I'm glad that you are going to stay in town.
I'm sorry that your success is going to limit our times
    together.
My success may be at other places and I must search,
    but I will focus nearby,
and maybe

                  I will find my own success here too.
                    But that will further limit
                        our times together.

I have trouble accepting and dealing with inevitability
        It gives me a fear that lives deep in my bones,
        and never lets go.
Inevitabilities,
like growing old, which used to mean
maturity and success to be celebrated at birthdays.
Birthdays that once celebrated survival and the wishful
    thinking toward another,
now no longer hold the excitement toward new
    accomplishments,
now mean disconnection of spirit and body,
a will no longer obeyed.
And the number of candles that once contained judgment
that favored us,
now questions us.

Inevitabilities,
like meeting and knowing wonderful people,
some that don't share the same feeling
who's relationship will never get to that place in spite
    of best efforts.
It is hard to accept and hard to deal with.
Hard to recognize that there is absolutely nothing more
    or different that can be
done to mitigate
the term "not feeling it".

Hard because I've been there before, on your side
with my head knowing its truth and inevitability.
Hard because my heart keeps an iron grip on hope
That maybe, somehow, a miracle will happen,
a hope that won't let go.
Hard because my bones ache in the fear that
no one will strike me like this again
or that there may be, but will also " not feel it."

Our time together is limited, always was, always will be.
Inevitably
But I love the times we have
The times as friends
It will fade, the time, as your success accelerates
As your new life with new job, new boyfriends, new health,
    new spirit
supernovas.
I recognized that potential.
I am lucky to have been there as the conditions aligned.

I hope I helped it happen.
That potential, I loved.
I knew its inevitability,
and I wish I was in there,
part of the glorious explosion
instead as an outside observer.
But as anyone that has witnessed anything so magnificent,
I am touched profoundly,
in a good way,
as your friend who does "feel it".
It was inevitable
and I'll deal with it the best I can.

I love you.

Hunger

There is so much, I need it
I seek it
Those words, those lovely long syllables that speak only to me
Not my words, the visionaries,'
Visionaries of so long ago, or only seems to be
Cause they started before I was born

Documentary videos with history, interviews
And snippets of wisdom.
With lists of the poets and artists
But only the famous
My soul yearns to hear
To absorb
To BE a part

And who shows me these places,
But the young that I envy for their youth
Not for the beauty, yet unfaded
But for the energy, for the extra years
For the genius to recognize the path so much earlier
Before I opened my eyes, my ears, my mind

I need eternal light, anti-bloodshot big-eyed firm focus
Quiet and jazz and comfort and time
Oh yes time
30 hours a day
9 days a week

5 weeks a month
and non-sleep slumber
instant absorption?

Time to ponder, but must read
Time to write, but must read

Maybe the key is in the words
The solution the help from the predecessors
Mr. Burroughs might have the bit
Mr. Ginsburg could point the way
Mr. Kerouac can only feed more of the hunger
Maybe it is here in the here-words
Words from Levy, Thompson, Crane, Hughes
Or the hereNnow words
Words from Smith, Lang, Ragain, McNiece
Or just maybe the hereNtomorrow words
Words from Malina, Sopko, Traenkner, Dyson,
    Grey-Kontar,
so many many more.

They all may show me how
Oh god, I'm back to where I started
I need more to find out how to get more
I'm starving, but what nourishes is what causes me hunger
Like a sip of ocean water that parches so much more

This
A new Beat
A new hippy

A new punk
Or just old samsaric living
in the hungry ghost realm.

Halim in My Dream

On the rough hewn wall
inside where grain and corn is stored,
words were scratched by a buckeye nut.
Laborers amble in
glancing up at the message.
Most shake their heads, muttering something like
"Damn kids."
Some stopped, stared, tried
make out the meaning.

Each day, a new scribbling
greeted with a similar response.
Though some that stared,
now barely paid any mind.
Some that muttered,
now stopped to look.

A week or more later,
lunch break
the usual African drum beats
from a small CD player,
complements from the eldest of the group,
remind most of home
before they came for the jobs.

The talk is, of course,
Who scratched these bewildering cyphers.

"Kids and hoodlums".
"Wiseguys trying to be cute"
Each accompanied by agreeing nods
as midday meals are chewed.

But when could they do it?
Since work usually starts at dawn,
lasts til past daybreak.
Kids have school,
hoodlums can't get past security,
only a short time to sneak in,
write big bold letters,
sneak out,
no guard-arousing noise.
It simply is not possible.

Quietly, The Elder suggests
It was from a god.
Who else is motivated
to give long suffering laborers
a message of hope?
Although how,
he is lost.

Then the youngest of the troupe
Still in his teens
Adds
"Unless he is here,
as one of us."

Every eye scanned every brow,
in anxious wonderment.
The Elder chewingly smiles,
and nods,
"Yes, yes if he is one of us."

My On The Road

On my road,
my neck is tight right down to the shoulders.
It spasms if I turn to the right or left.
On my road,
the left eye twitches trying to close for a while
during the lonely long drive.
On my road,
sleep is a memory used as a reward
if only to survive just a little while longer.
On my road,
high tech phones rattle and buzz incessantly
with messages of bad news.
On my road,
ignorant customers compensate by complaining
until they leave for their comfortable home,
abandoning me to complete another 12 hour day.
On my road,
the clocks tick too fast at night
and too quickly towards deadlines during the day.
On my road,
food is plentiful and heavy,
available only at odd hours
and distastefully returns during the night.
On my road,
maps send me to isolated towns in isolated states in
    isolated countries
where shopping malls are cultural centers
and taverns are churches.

On my road,
I walk into walls during nocturnal piss runs
because I don't remember which city or hotel I'm in.
On my road,
hotel beds are too firm and lack a cradling hole
like the one home,
carefully formed over years of
patient idleness.
On my road,
insomnia is my one true companion, the reliable friend
always there in the emptiness of a lonely hotel room.
On my road,
even dreams are projects and
rest drags a heavy tool bag.

In my On The Road story,
there is no Moriarty, no Paradise,
no adventure, no self-discovery,
no kicks, no Beat.
Only the monotonous drone of a dissipating soul.

Beershit Sure

Buk said it's natural, like taking a good beer shit.
But I run around the apartment listening to weird mellow
music from Peru and cloistered monks falsetto
in hundred year old chants to Jesus.
I stick my head out the window and let the rain hit
as if each drop would pound a word into it.
I nosh on ice cream and spicy sunflower seeds, thinking the
ice cream is good fertilizer and maybe the seeds will take
root and blossom with verse.
I disturb my lovely companion with my dancing flutters
and flail to find something to type. So far. she has
met the first and foremost requirement in my imaginary
classified ad, "extremely tolerant"
Fertilizer is like shit only purified
and only heartburn comes from the seeds.
I am still constipated and urban
spring will have to sprung without a touching description
from me. Sorry, Hank, you are full of' shit.
Writing is not as easy and natural as a good beer shit.
But when it happens, it sure as hell feels as good.
Til then, I'll go annoy my sweetheart some more and
see how tolerant she really is.

All Talk

On the first warm day near spring
while sitting out at an urban café's sidewalk table
by the big park,
I told my dear companion that
this
would make a great poem.

In a recently discovered local hideaway,
I said while sharing a chocolate mousse
that this place is rife with poems.
Perhaps to be written at the small table
near the bathroom toward the end of the bar,
where Valery, the waitress,
has to squeeze by,
holding gourmet pizzas.

I interrupt myself during pillow talk
the morning after beautiful love making
to say I should write this stuff down.
It would make a tremendous poem.

I dream about what it would have been like
if I expatriated to Paris after the Great War
and sat at the cafes
and danced at the nightclubs
with my fellow Americans, the artists.

I wonder if I would say after sipping an espresso
with Scott Fitzgerald that this view
would make a nice poem.
Or ask Pablo if I can write
something on his latest piece.

I wonder if Ernie Hemingway
would shake his head
after I left and tell Gertie Stein,
"There goes another one.
If only he wrote the good poem
instead of telling us what
would be a good poem,
he just might become something."

Then they would all separate to make beautiful art.

Lost In Sandusky

On a Sunday's afternoon,
squinting stares at faded street signs
and Mapquest ambiguity on the passenger seat
Block by Block
a great lake ahead
tardy poems turn to panic swallowed
and Mother telling me about
GPS on the cellphone.

Las Palomas

In the early morning
they swoop to the top step
of the pool where
humans splash and lounge all day.
But now early
before the sun heats the day
as the humans are still sleeping in beds
holding their heads from the night before
the proud birds land, strut, and splash
cooling and cooing.
In NY they are called rats with wings
but in the dust of Mexico
each takes a turn to
sit and dip
maybe take a sip.

A large, beautifully plumed pigeon
sat overlooking the small flock
Another, when it was his turn
would stretch out a wing and roll
onto his back and flap and splash
in adolescent frivolity until another
would butt him out of the way.
Sometimes it would turn into a free-for-all
until Big Daddy would hop into the middle
squat down to cool his legs
then wing spread splash the others off the platform
into deeper water.

Only when crows
with large tails and matching beaks
come for a drink and a rinse,
does Big Daddy make way
But it is a share, much like the
bustle of moped, golf cart, auto, and people
on the narrow boulevard.
In time, the ebony feathered gargantuans leave
and the water dance
continues like there was no interruption
until they are scattered by the approaching
maid, going to pick red flowers
from the surrounding bushes
that later, I will find festooning
a bird of twisted towels
on my hotel bed.

It's Always 3 O' Clock

when I look at the clock.
The clock isn't broken, no, not stopped
with arms up and out like a traffic cop
It is just 3 o' clock
every time I first glance up
and the better part of the day is past.
The sun is on its downward dip to the horizon.
Blood sugar hangs low.

In the frig, once fresh herbs
bright and pungent quickly turn dark, slimy, furred with mold.
Fresh paint peels from wood molding along floorboards
    and windows.
The fresh scrubbed tub has mold in its grout.
The living room carpet prairie has tumbleweed lint balls
    rolling in the furnace wind.
Polished shelves show mouse tracks in its dust.
Frayed collars jump out from the latest laundry and socks
    need mending
as if anyone still did that anymore.

What can't be scrubbed, wiped, vac'd, or fixed
must be replaced.
It all depends on how hard the work
and how much time remains.
My body creaks with surprising volume,
its noon not so long past.

When I have a job Time flys by.
When I have a routine Time flys by.
When I don't have either Time flys by.

I'm in the three o' clock of my life
and it's three o' clock in the afternoon.
I need lots of work,
and dusk is coming quickly.

I'll Miss Cleveland, If I Must

(Note: kunuku is Papiamento for an island country village
or hideaway)

If I leave this place, this Cleveland
of tuck-a-way neighborhoods,
of rusty urban landscapes and cornucopic gardens,
a place of the fat and the lean
a place of the poor and the rich,

I will miss its cafes' hard metal chairs
and hard metal tables
that rock with any slight imbalance
as discussions lean from losing sport teams
to new experimental rock groups and art openings.

I'll miss the short walks from my inexpensive apartment
amidst the gentrified heralds of luxury;
foreign cars and enormous SUVs
too large for streets mottled with potholes,
exposed brick and cobble that were built
for horses, carriages, and the occasional pushcart.

I'll miss those walks to a park
once known as a needle playground
for junkies and their pushers,
where now world class dance companies
whorl to classics, and jazz,
and avant garde noises

with body gestures, smooth
in their evening air synchronization,
and where Shakespeare is modernized to hipsters
performed around a gazebo that still shelters
the homeless during the late nights.
And opera rings around idle smokestacks
blending ancient tragedy with the recent.

I'll miss saying hello to all my canine friends
that may only love me for the morsels I share
while their owners nod acquiescence
but hold the leashes tight with smiles
that match their dogs' simaculum
that tolerate my touch on their soft, soft fur,
the adequate replica of companionship.

I'll miss the private back garden at the neighborhood
bar, only open 3 nights a week. The trendy popular bars also
have patios to serve their patrons' lust for al fresco.
But here, there is no blaring music and you can
    contemplate
the setting sun and the color of flowers that grow
over the graves of family cats and the ashes of a
    famous poet.
It is just a hideaway, a kunuku, in a rustbelt island.
Serve yourself in the blue collar way.

And I'll miss my balcony
where if I'm to be alone, I like to be alone there
with a fresh roast-and-brew or homemade mojito
looking North at the city skyline,

remembering all the poems written in that self same place
wondering where is the source of all those words.
Is it a dry pit since they don't flow anymore?

These things fashion a finely woven lace, twenty years
    in the making
each memory, a thin delicate thread
strong for their size, especially if pulled or twisted the
    right way
but still tenuous and fragile,
easily broken if the wrong tug comes
from the wrong direction.
But enough of them, together, wrapped around each other
one's weak point, protected by another's strong point,
deflects the tension to other helping threads,
each accepting what it can handle.
It forms a massive doily of ropes and cables
strong without bound,
yet retaining the beauty of the basic elements.

A fish net of smiles and handshakes,
that gleans sweet oysters out of turbulent seas
and feed them to a hungry mouth,
then decorate the sorrowful tear with the pearls.
A dome of hugs and kisses,
that shields us from the launched missiles of life.
A pillow of fond remembrance
that cushions us from blindsided concussions.
It is a safety net stretched across a chasm of despair
as we lunge and stumble blindly, reaching out
for some silly concept of progress.

It is a harness that catches us and stands us up.
It swaddles us in a protective embrace
and then lets us go when we are ready, to make our
    own mistakes.
It is a bandage that binds the wounds that inevitably come.

This I will miss most of all.
It is a difficult thing to make, to keep,
It feeds on us as much as we feed on it,
It can reach as far as the universe, if it is maintained.

And so it may be time to go somewhere else
and rely on this lace, trust it to help
to use what was learned in its making to make another
to see if the new will blend with the old
and see if will be seamless, or just a new pattern
to hope that it will be as strong and as soft as before.

This, I will miss along with the ice cream, the baseball
    fireworks,
friendly waves on the street, and the round of
drinks from a former stranger.

In the same the same park that hosts on Tuesdays
a farmers market
where urban farmers, suburban farmers, Amish farmers
and raisers of livestock sell their goods as of pre-industrial
    days,
with guitars playing, and gossip swapped, and vendors
    offering
pizza and pierogies and maybe hemp cookies.

It is wisdom and silliness,
prescribed in the right proportions
and administered at the right times.
It is a compass to show our disoriented spirit the correct way,
or at least the best way.

Hafiz in a Hurricane

Power is out, blown away by
the magnificent storm,
only a tip of nature's finger touching our lives.
An interruption to helter-skelter existence
made up by feeble minds.

Man-made caves that block the sky
and isolate us
is dark.
Only outside is light enough
to illuminate the soul.
Light enough
to read
The Gift
from Hafiz.

Windblown spray penetrates
the porch corner to a chair.
Droplets make pages sticky to the Touch.
They fill my Well to overflowing,
Even as my outstretched arm holds
a cup offered
but ignored by neighbors
as they drive by in a rush,
futilely seeking
the happiness they can't believe
could be contained
in such a tiny vessel.

Greatness

The thing about knots is that
if they can be tied,
they can be untied.

Alexander was a coward to cut the Gordian knot,
for the sake of expediency, he made the rope unusable
The knot was not useful,
the rope was.
And so his vast empire was short lived.
And after his death, like the knot,
was no longer useful
leaving so many
small
ineffectual
rope
remnants.

Just think what could have been,
if only he took the time
to unravel the Gordian knot.
What a long
and strong
rope that would have been.

Gourmands in the House

My ex-wife
Is furiously allergic
Dust, she says
In her regurgitated doctor over-simplification
Said in that 28 year naturalized Puerto Rican accent.

Geek as I am, I researched
Google gollies dust allergies
As dust MITE allergies
But not dust mites
But dust mite FECES
Yup microscopic organism shit
She's allergic
Who wouldn't be

Apparently not dust mites
See, if our dead skin flakes
Can't sate their hunger
Mighty mites munch
Their own crap

I wonder
Do they sauté
Or marinate
with sweat-salt
To hide the overly familiar redundant taste

They are not allergic
I want to be.

Good Will to Some Men

Tis the season for pine scented allergies
and eggnogged noggins.
People start to blink in time with the
plastic tree lites. Depending on
how they sync
it is all brite
or all dark.
Either way they don't
see the heathen suffer.

Freedom

Time is abundant
Time is infinite
Time is mine once again
Time to sit on a balcony
> to watch a huge new moon in the clear crisp
> winter night
All night.
Dancing to the chimes
of wage slave chains
falling away forever.

So with this freedom,
You may want to know what I'm doing.
Well, I'll tell ya.
> I'm having a hotdog.
> The most delicious hotdog.

Eventually

I sit cross legged trying to acquire
The grand perfection of patience.
Hum through the tingling numbness in folded ankles,
being Patient.
Waiting to just get over with it.

Patience is a virtue,
is the lack of anger,
is equanimity of pleasant outlook
It's looking out with slight smile
and confidence
knowing that all changes
That it is all good.
or will be
Eventually.

I try to remind myself
as thoughts turn to a year ago
when a yoga instructor
enchanted me, but wasn't ready.
There was so much to carry
but she didn't have change in her purse
to tip the valet.
The baggage would move, by van
or by garbage truck,
eventually.

I never imagined she would continue
to lug it herself, ignoring my
offers of help.
I had to be patient
for her to come on her own
eventually.

I could not shave Time's long beard
until it grew out a bit more
Maybe she worried that my beer belly
would shake a hand and cut a throat.
So she accepted someone else's offer.
Now, I hope my desire will bleed out
And only friendship will remain.
And it will all be good
eventually.

Beach Buddhist

Rejuvenation rhymes with the roar of the waves.
Each step on the sand puts a grain of wisdom between toes,
the sound of cycles blow into one nostril and out the other,
There is no one else on the beach.
There are footsteps ahead
and behind.
Are they mine? Were they mine?
Will they be mine for the next beachcomber?
What does it matter, I am here, now.

I look across the water to see France, but they don't recognize me.
I turn 5 degrees to the right and don't see
the surviving Africans as they stare out toward me.
On one end of the beach, there is only more beach to the
    horizon.
On the other end, there is a pier with windmills waving at me.
I start to walk toward the welcoming arms.

And so the sand starts scouring away my ego
from the soles of my feet
and up to the soul of my being.
Each step, becomes more isolating
Each step becomes more connecting.
Evidence of death in calcium shell are memorials to the
    struggle.
The salt air is the promise of life.

Lazy swirling bands of dakinis keep an eye, I think,
on my journey, but then
swoop down on unsuspecting fishlike maras,
or poke at the holes in the sand for a sweet clam delight.
Another bruise on my need-to-be-battered ego.

The pier is full of rods hanging over the side
like mutated spider legs.
Web lines dropping into the sea to snare some suffering.
Grumblers, unsmiling, look out to the surf and back to
     their empty coolers.
A few have caught sand sharks.
I saw one removing his hook from a clear nose skate.
They dumped them over the side, as the law requires.
I was secretly happy for their frustration and hoped
     eventually
they would develop an enjoyment of setting living things
     free
after feeding them little snacks.

Clear eyed crows stand sentinel in case a morsel gets
dropped near them. They are the protectors.
If you can lock eyes with one you can see the intrinsic
     wisdom inside.
Only a rescued pitbull was happy to see me
and he sat on my foot until I rubbed his head enough.

I set on my path back and noticed my trail has been
     erased
by the coming tide.

With every wave that washed across my feet,
it took away anger, jealousy, hatred, desire
and fed the swimming plankton bodhisattvas in my new mind.
With every breath of the sea air, i pulled in goodness, compassion,
a wish for the betterment of those across the water.
Step by step, breath by breath, wave by wave
I discovered the beach lojong,
and i felt cleansed, renewed, pure.
My only witness was huge fat old seagull,
squatting in a huge man's footprint in the sand,
protected from the wind,
and i knew from its half lidded eyes, he was a Buddha.

And the ocean with its creatures, big and small,
their deaths and their lives,
was samsara.
Yet its tide was the promise of enlightenment
and finally you realize that it is the same thing.

A Talent for Madness

(for Brin Metzendorf) *from *A Talented Mind* by William Burkholter

The lens of perception takes a strange tint.
Not dark or black,
more twisted, like a funhouse mirror.
Simple defeats take on magnified importance
but victories of kindness
an extra quarter tip to a waitress
a dog licking a hand
a cup of coffee, gratis from an old barista friend
are shrunk to a minute speck, under the notice
of even a fly's compound eyesight.

I read a dead poet's works in admiration
and forget how he took his own life.
So many works I admire
seem to be from victims of their own hand
a few extra pills
a long walk off a short pier
pockets full of rocks
a stove burner left on.

I remember the happy sarcasm and open generosity
of a Mad Bunny. Self taught musician,
with jamming licks.
An actor that made us cry about happiness.
A writer who put soul into syllables and
let them fly.

Decided he wasn't alone enough in a
rural farmhouse.
Said goodbye to us all.

Another poet wrote:*
"He made a shotgun rendering
of a talented mind"
I think sometimes of a story I read
about Arab assassins that used
extremely thin knife blades, super sharp.
They slid between the 2nd and 3rd cervical
vertebrae like rain through a cloud.
Done to victims in their sleep
no pain, no mess
just slumber without ever a yawn.

I can't do that to myself
I'm not smart enough nor talented enough.

From My Perch

From my perch, I can see so much.

I can see the tops of skyscrapers filled with struggling
businesses.

I can see the flies lighting on cat crap.

I can see the wind flutter thru the war vet's flag.

I can see Old Blind Dog and his lifelong buddy,
Old Deaf Dog lounge in the sun.

I can see a Cadillac take the alley shortcut.

I can see a mound of mulch that replaced the dying
hollow tree.

I can see the empty parking spot, signally a few short
hours of stressless tranquility

I can see four teenage girls with blossoming curves,
strut to the corner mart.

I can see the four old hillbilly friends sharing their
loneliness thru political talk.

I can see so many satellite dishes that promise the
world and only deliver the banal.

I can see a robin slip thru the siding to build a nest in
my eave.

and I can see the coming end of my quiet balcony time
where I can see so much.

Easter

I celebrate Easter with a hangover
while I check my boxers for skidmarks
and wait for a resurrection.
The best I can hope for is picking olives out
of a garden salad of Eden
bought by a King of the Jews
from Mountainview.
Nocturnal madness explodes into quiet rooms
in the form of lisping gayness and friends.
Their inside voice rattles rain from the skies
and an egoless commercial actor fakes an injury
just to get a night off from work.
Shy guard dogs aggressively retreat,
barking and snarling bravado
as they enter their crate.
In spite of broken world records,
daylight isn't saved for sleep or a Chagall painting,
Nevertheless, the train will leave very early in the fog.

Ear Hair

Hair wakes me
with tickles that make my ear sneeze.
They grow without invitation.
Weeds nourished by bullshit
I've been forced to hear.
That is why they sprout now.
Late into middle age
They tickle with whispered
reminders of advancing age.
As if aching hips, gray hair, and bulging belly
aren't reminders enough.
But at least those let me sleep through the night.

For J

An online picture shows the last time I saw J,
which was the last time I was in Oakland.
At the time I knew I would be back in Oakland someday.
In the same way, I thought I would see J someday.
More than ever, I wish I wasn't wrong.

Steve Goldberg has been part of the Cleveland poetry scene for longer than anyone expected. Steve has been published in many of Cleveland's small press zines and is included in the book *Cleveland Poetry Scenes: A Panorama & Anthology* (Bottom Dog Press) and the coffee table book, *Hotel Poem, Poets of Cleveland* (Language Foundry) . His chapbook, *Tremont Crawl*, sold out in its third printing. He has read all across the country and participated in poetry festivals such as Kansas City's Unregulated Word, Oakland's Beast Crawl, the Tremont Art and Cultural Festival, and has been the MC for Rainy Day in Seattle poetry festival. As a poetry event organizer, Steve led the legendary Literary Café Reading Series for four years, the bombastic Metrical Singularity Supernova festival, and Broken Pulpit poetry weekend and crawl in Cleveland.

CPSIA information can be obtained
at www.ICGtesting.com
Printed in the USA
BVHW081502210921
617187BV00008B/394